AWFULLY ANCIENT

Banished, Beheaded, or Boiled in Oil

A Hair-Raising History of Crime and Punishment Throughout the Ages!

Neil Tonge

Gareth Stevens
PUBLISHING

Please visit our website, **www.garethstevens.com**.
For a free color catalog of all our high-quality books,
call toll-free 1-800-542-2595 or fax 1-877-542-2596.

Library of Congress Cataloging-in-Publication Data

Tonge, Neil.
Banished, beheaded, or boiled in oil: a hair-raising history of crime
and punishment throughout the ages! / by Neil Tonge.
p. cm. — (Awfully ancient)
Includes index.
ISBN 978-1-4824-3121-6 (pbk.)
ISBN 978-1-4824-3124-7 (6 pack)
ISBN 978-1-4824-3122-3 (library binding)
1. Crime — History — Juvenile literature. 2. Punishment — History —
Juvenile literature. 3. Criminals — History — Juvenile literature.
I. Tonge, Neil. II. Title.
HV6027.T58 2016
364.9—d23

Published in 2016 by
Gareth Stevens Publishing
111 East 14th Street, Suite 349
New York, NY 10003

Copyright © 2016 Wayland / Gareth Stevens

Senior editor: Julia Adams
Illustrator: Tom Morgan-Jones
Designer: Rocket Design (East Anglia) Ltd.

Manufactured in the United States of America
CPSIA compliance information: Batch #CS15GS.
For further information contact Gareth Stevens, New York, New York at 1-800-542-2595.

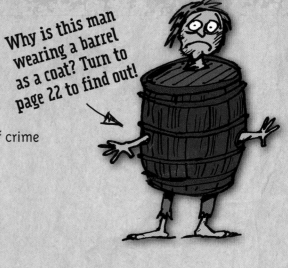

Why is this man wearing a barrel as a coat? Turn to page 22 to find out!

Yes, that is a lady stuck under a door. Page 21 will tell you why.

Ah, the Chelsea Pensioner; that well-respected old fellow of London town... Or is it? Find out more on page 26.

Contents

What happens at your school if you do something wrong? Do you have to hold out your hands so your teacher can whip them with a switch, as was the case in Victorian times? When you misbehave at home, are you banished (sent to live in a faraway place) as you might have been in Roman times? Would you expect to have your hand chopped off if you wrote rude words about the queen, as might have happened in Elizabethan times? No. At worst you might get told off, have to eat ALL your greens and be banned from watching TV.

To be fair, misbehaving isn't criminal behavior, but we can still all be glad that many forms of punishment today are far less gruesome than they used to be...

In the past, there have been some amazing achievements by ancient civilizations — the ancient Egyptians and Aztecs built stunning pyramids, China drew up the Great Wall, the Greeks produced formidable thinkers, and the Romans were engineering geniuses!

On April 5, 1531, Richard Roose was boiled to death after confessing to poisoning 17 people.

Not just vegetables, sprouts!

BUT when it came to criminals, they all had some stomach-churning, not-so-civilized ways of dealing with them.

In this book, we are going to roll up our sleeves and delve right into the history of terrible tortures, putrid punishments and excruciating executions.

Fetch the sack and find me a lion!

Here's a little taster for you...

Try to bribe a government official in Roman times and you were likely to have your nose cut off, be tied in a sack with a wild animal (it's not specified what sort, but you can bet it wasn't the cuddly kind) and then thrown off a cliff.

Arghhh!

Do you get the idea? This book is not for the faint-hearted...

Grrrrrr!

Chilling China

Oooo, scratch my nose..

Our first stop on the gruesome trail of crime and punishment is ancient China. Qin Shi Huang (pronounced *Kwin – She – Wang*) became the first emperor of a united China in 221 BCE. Before Qin's time, China had been a patchwork of squabbling kingdoms. Once united, the Chinese Empire lasted for a staggering 2,132 years before it was finally swept away in a revolution in 1911.

Despite the wide-reaching powers of the Emperor, accused criminals did have some rights.

Cangue – naming and shaming!

Imagine having a large wooden board, weighing 22 pounds (10 kg), fastened around your neck. So large, in fact, that you couldn't bring food or drink to your mouth. This was one of the ways of punishing the accused in ancient China. The board, or cangue, was also used to post the offender's crime, name, and address. And you thought privacy was an Internet-era issue...

Guilty or not guilty?

Before punishment was exercised, the accused got a chance to confess the crime. Then, if they didn't, torture was used to encourage them to confess. The main form of torture was beating the suspect on the soles of their feet with a big stick.

Once found guilty, what happened next? Then it got pretty nasty. If you'd committed really serious crimes then you could be...

Boiled alive

China has some of the earliest accounts of boiling prisoners to death in water or oil. During the process, the victim suffered high-degree burns, their skin was gradually destroyed and they basically fried to death. Lil-chi (203 BCE) was one such unfortunate sautéed victim. He was sent on a diplomatic peace mission, only to discover that, while talks were going on, the official who sent him decided to attack the peace party. Lil-chi was considered a traitor and deep-fried to death...

Flayed alive

Ever scraped your skin? Stings, doesn't it? Now imagine having ALL your skin removed. And that's what flaying involved. In this delightful ancient Chinese practice, the victim was skinned alive as part of a public execution, after which the skin was nailed to a wall as a warning to others. And on this stinging subject, Emperor Sun Hao (242–284 CE) personally removed the skin from the faces of his victims. What a nice chap.

Don't worry – you'll be fried to a crisp in no time...

Gruesome Greeks

800 BCE – 600 CE

Defiantly dedicated

Spartan children who stole were very dedicated to the cause. In one recorded case, a boy, having stolen a young fox and hidden it under his cloak, let the fox viciously attack him. The boy died of the wounds, rather than being found out.

In ancient times, Greece was divided into a number of squabbling city-states, of which the most important were Athens and Sparta. In about 620 BCE, Draco, an Athenian, wrote the first known legal code in ancient Greece. And what was the first law he set? The punishment for murder was to be sent into exile. The Greeks felt that being banished from Greek civilization was worse than death!

Draco getting a warm welcome!

Ooof!

Law and order

The Greeks had courts, but there were no lawyers or judges. The accused and accuser would argue the matter out, and then a "jury" would decide on the verdict. There was no limit to the number of jurors, and one recorded trial had as many as 1,000! To be a juror, you had to be at least 30 years old and a male citizen of Athens.

Sentences were based on Draco's legal code, which basically stated that all crimes (apart from murder) should be punished by death. According to legend, in 620 BCE, the famous lawgiver met a very unusual end. He was smothered to death by gifts of hats and cloaks that were showered down on him from admirers in the audience of a theater at Aegina.

Savage Sparta

Not all Greek city-states believed all crimes were wrong. The city-state of Sparta was one such place. Nowadays parents usually tell their children that stealing is wrong, but the good Spartan parents said just the opposite. They expected their children to steal in order to survive, and, of course, not to get caught.

A load of bull?

Some ancient Greek city-states devised their very own nasty endings for criminals. Take the "brazen bull," for example. This was a huge, hollow bronze bull with a door. The prisoner was shut inside, and then a fire was lit underneath, turning the metal white-hot and roasting the person to death. The head of the bull was built with a system of tubes, so when the victim screamed, the noise that was made sounded like an angry bull; hence the name.

Aaaaaaar-ghhhhhhhh!

The brazen bull

(A particularly nasty invention)

It's All Greek to Me!

A Greek Trial

A very old scratchcard

Democratic voting scratchcard (men only)

CANDIDATE A ☐

CANDIDATE B ☐

CANDIDATE C ☐

Banish the Brazen Bull Party ☐

Scratch chosen box with a cross

Athens was the largest and richest city in ancient Greece. They did not have kings, but instead allowed the men of Athens to vote for who they wanted to run the government. We call this system a democracy. ("demos" = people and "cracy" = government). Democracy, as a form of government, was eventually to spread around the world.

As we now know, Athens had juries of ordinary people (well, ordinary men) deciding who was guilty and how he or she should be punished. So when it came to crime and punishment, things should have been quite fair, shouldn't they? Let's look at one of the most famous trials in history to see how just this system really was...

Hmmm

Errr...

The case of Socrates (399 BCE)

Socrates was one of the most famous men in Athens. He was a philosopher and teacher. He encouraged his students to think for themselves. "Keep asking questions," he told them, "What is justice? If the gods exist, where do they live?" Not everyone was happy with this.

The crime To the rich Athenians he appeared to be a troublemaker, stirring up discontent. So they put him on trial for turning young men's minds against the gods. This was no light matter, as the punishment, if found guilty, was death.

The trial Socrates couldn't take the charge seriously and thought it so ridiculous that he refused to defend himself. (Remember, there were no lawyers or judges in an Athenian court). As he wouldn't deny the charges, the jury found him guilty.

The jury were a bit embarrassed by it all, though, so they asked Socrates what sort of punishment he should suffer. "What about a fine of one piece

of silver," he suggested sarcastically. The jury were furious. If this clever guy was not going to respect them, then he left them with no choice but to condemn him to death. The jury voted for death by 280 votes to 220, but gave him the choice of how he was to die.

The sentence Socrates chose to drink a cup of hemlock, a deadly poison.

Well, at least he wasn't roasted or deep-fried...

Revolting Romans

500 BCE – 400 CE

It's a tough life in the army. If the enemy doesn't kill you, there's a good chance your mates will!

The Romans had a superb, well-disciplined army and conquered a vast empire that lasted from 27 BCE to 476 CE. You can rest assured that they did not manage this by being the nice guys. Above all, they made sure that their legionaries obeyed orders. But what if they didn't?

Atteeeeention!

Run away from the enemy in battle, then you were stoned to death or beaten to death in front of the army. Steal from your mates and you could be tied up in a sack with snakes for company and thrown into a river. Disobey an order and you were flogged. This wasn't just a simple whipping — the skin on your back would be left hanging off like a pair of ragged curtains.

Unlike these days, winning the X Factor was bad news in Roman times.

If the whole legion didn't fight well enough, then every tenth man was beaten to death by his mates. This was known as "decimation" ("deci" means ten). Some mates!

The "X" Factor

If the Romans were hard on their soldiers, they were just as tough on civilians. Crucifixion was a favored and an agonizing death for criminals. The victim was nailed to a cross. The nails were driven through their wrists and heels to support the "dead" weight of the body. Eventually, as their strength seeped away, they could not lift their chest to breathe and suffocated. If no one claimed the body, it was thrown on a trash heap for wild animals to snack on.

Strangulation was a quicker and slightly less brutal way to go. It was carried out in a form known as "garrotting." A cord was placed around the neck, and then twisted until it crushed the throat and the eyes popped. That's what happened to Vercingetorix, the defeated leader of the Gauls, in 46 BCE.

GULP!

ENTERTAINMENT – ROMAN STYLE

The deaths of criminals were sometimes given an extra twist by putting them on as entertainment in the arenas. In some cases it was just plain brutal; other times they dressed the event up in honor of a great Roman hero. One of the audience favorites was Mucius Scaevola (508 BCE), who proved his bravery by sticking his hand in a fiery brazier until it burned clean away. Roman spectators craved gaudy executions such as being burnt alive, dragged to death behind horses, or torn to pieces by wild beasts.

Awful Aztecs

1400 – 1550 CE

Let's have a peek at punishment in a completely different part of the world: The Americas. The Aztecs, who lived in what is now Mexico, were a tribe of North American natives who built an extraordinary and far-reaching civilization. They erected huge pyramids, were very successful farmers and ruled over a vast empire that stretched from the Gulf of Mexico to the Pacific Ocean.

Smoking hot

When Aztec teenagers misbehaved, they were forced to inhale the smoke of burning chillies. This caused burns to the nose, eyes and mouth.

Altar-native punishment

Having conquered many settlements to build up their empire, the Aztecs were hardly likely to be soft on criminals. Their courts were ruled over by warriors who decided the punishment, which could range from fines to death.

For less serious crimes you might endure your house being pulled down, or have your head shaved.

Nuts!

If found guilty of theft, you were fined the value of what had been stolen; for injuries, the cost of tending to the wounds of the injured party. If you were involved in kidnapping or handling stolen goods, you were sold into slavery for a fixed period of time.

If pronounced guilty of a more severe crime, such as murder, the criminal was taken to a nearby altar and stoned or strangled. Aztecs believed crimes were committed against the gods, so punishment was carried out in a place of worship.

Confess your crime

There was one way out of punishment, but you had to be quick. If you confessed your crime to the priests of Tlazolteotl before you were caught, you would be forgiven. But only if you were a first-time offender. Repeat the crime, and you were punished — probably by death.

No, it wasn't your identical twin. I'm pretty sure it was you...

Getting the point

The Aztecs had many interesting ways of punishing naughty children. Break anything or be rude, then you might be tied up outside the house through the night. Boys sometimes had a cactus needle pushed into their skin. Girls were usually punished by having to do a large amount of household chores.

Murderous Middle Ages

5th – 15th century

Anyone in the stocks became the perfect target for some rotten eggs...

In the Middle Ages, it wasn't just about punishing the crime — torture, in order to make the accused confess, became a refined art. A number of handy little devices were developed along the way...

Ghastly gadgets

The "head crusher" was a popular torture device in Medieval times. It consisted of a metal cap that was pressed down on the victim's head, which in turn rested on a metal bar. This splintered the teeth and the jaw.

The "knee crusher" consisted of two rows of metal spikes placed above and below the knee and then tightened with a screw. Last but certainly not least, the "Spanish donkey" was particularly horrid: the victim sat astride a pyramid–shaped block; then weights were attached to their legs until they began to split in two. Medieval folk were SUCH a nice bunch.

Punishment

If you chose to admit the crime, rather than prove your innocence (see opposite), you were either locked in the stocks — a wooden structure in which the hands and neck were secured — or you were hanged. This involved being strung up by the neck and slowly strangled. If the victim was fortunate, relatives were allowed to pull their legs to shorten the agony.

They really didn't mess about in Medieval times...

WHAT AN ORDEAL!

Welcome! As a Medieval defendant you get one last chance to prove your innocence...

ORDEAL BY WATER

To prove you are innocent, you will be tied up in a sack and thrown into water. If you float, you are guilty of the crime you were accused of, because no one could float without the help of the devil. But if you sink, you will be declared innocent. One slight problem: if you sink, you're also probably dead...

ORDEAL BY FIRE

Hold a red-hot iron bar and walk three paces. Then your hand will be bandaged and left for three days. If the wound gets better after three days, you are innocent. If the wound turns red and inflamed and oozes slimy stuff, then obviously you are guilty.

> Urgh. This is DEFINITELY hotter than a slice of toast...

ORDEAL BY COMBAT

What more civilized way of settling a dispute than having a good scrap? This form of trial by ordeal (for insult, injury or theft) is reserved for the nobility. Square up to one another with weapons and clobber each other until the guilty one is dead.

Curious Cases of Criminal Creatures

Pet prison

In 1712, an Austrian pet dog was sentenced to a year in jail because he bit a councilman on the leg. The dog shared its jail cell with two human inmates.

In the Middle Ages, Europeans put animals — pigs, goats, sheep and even rats — on trial, often providing them with all the same rights as people, including the right to a lawyer and a fair trial.

Criminal pigs

Medieval pigs always seemed to get into trouble. In one such case in Falaise, France, a pig was hanged for attacking and killing a child. Her six piglets, however, who were also accused of taking part in the crime, were let off the charge because they were too young and the mother had obviously set a bad example. Before the pig's execution, the animal was dressed

You'll hang for this, you swine!

18

in a coat, gloves, trousers, and human mask. In another case, in 1379, two herds of pigs attacked and killed a swineherd's son. The judge sentenced both herds to death because although the first herd was responsible, the other herd had obviously enjoyed the experience by "squealing" with delight.

> You tell 'em!

> The safety of my clients cannot be guaranteed.

Animal attorney

The pigs were not only entitled to a fair trial, they even had lawyers to represent them. One such lawyer, Bartholomew Chassenee, gained a huge reputation by defending animals. In his most famous case, in 1522, he represented some rats who were charged with devouring a storage of barley in Burgundy, France.

> And don't come back!

He tried to delay the trial as long as possible so that the judge and jury might grow tired of the proceedings and drop the charges. On one occasion, he argued that there were too many cats in the town and the safety of his "clients" could not be guaranteed.

On the run

In 1519, a judge in Glurns, Italy, ordered mice to leave the district, but gave them safe conduct so they would not be harmed by cats and dogs. As a further concession, pregnant and infant mice could take an extra 14 days before they were forced to leave.

Church courts

Even the Church condemned the actions of animals. Many wild creatures found guilty by church courts were excommunicated (exiled from the church), for example when birds or rabbits ate farmers' crops. In 1474, a church court in Switzerland condemned a cockerel to be burned at the stake for the unnatural crime of laying an egg.

1519 saw a high number of mouse emigrations...

Terrifying Tudors

I'll draw him...

...and I'll quarter 'im.

The Tudors were a Welsh–English family that ruled England and Wales from 1485 to 1603. England became a rich and powerful nation during the reigns of the Tudor monarchs, and they dealt swiftly and nastily with anyone who upset them.

Rack and religion

Religion really, REALLY mattered in Tudor times. You were expected to have the same religion as your monarch, otherwise you were regarded as disloyal. Protestants and Catholics were at odds, to put it mildly, and if it was suspected that you were of the wrong religion, nasty times lay ahead.

Enter the torturer. His favorite instrument was the rack — a long table with rollers attached to each end. Anyone who was arrested for being of the "wrong" religion was tied to the rollers by rope. Then the rollers were turned until the accused screamed out the names of any fellow "religious traitors."

Hanging, drawing, and quartering

This was the punishment carried out in England for plotting against the monarch. The accused were hanged, but when they were still alive — and possibly conscious — they were cut down. The executioner then sliced open their stomach and "drew out" their intestines, kidneys and liver. Finally, the victim was beheaded and their body cut into quarters.

Do you feel like a chat at all?

REVOLTING RELIGION

Thomas Cranmer (March 12, 1556, Oxford)

Cranmer was the Protestant Archbishop of Canterbury when Catholic "Bloody" Mary was queen of England. He was arrested and after torture he signed a "confession" to say he had been wrong in his beliefs. Later, however, he renounced his confession. He was condemned to be burned at the stake. As the flames licked up his body, he held his right hand in the fire – the hand that had signed the confession.

Margaret Clitheroe (March 25, 1586, York)

Clitheroe had sheltered Catholic priests in her house; as Queen Elizabeth was Anglican, Clitheroe was declared a traitor. She was stripped and tied to the ground, face upwards. A large, sharp stone was pushed under her back, and then a heavy door laid on top of her. Stone weights were then placed on top of the door. As the pressure increased, Clitheroe, unable to breathe, groaned a last prayer.

Troubled Times

Not only were there threats from foreign countries and religious quarrels at home, but there was an increase in the number of poor people during Tudor times.

Paupers and punishments

There was no welfare state, so any poor people who became incapable of working had three options: beg, steal, or die. The way Henry VIII dealt with his subjects' poverty was to enforce harsh punishments for begging and stealing.

Charge Sheet

BEGGING

1st offense: whipped to the boundary of one's parish.

2nd offense: branded with the letter "V" for "vagabond" using a red-hot iron, or having an ear cut off.

3rd offense: hanged.

NAGGING

Only women were accused of this crime. The brank, a large iron framework, was placed on the head of the woman, forming a type of cage. A pointed metal strip fit into the mouth; the tongue would be pierced with the slightest movement.

DRUNKENNESS

For being drunk in a public place, the guilty could be placed in the stocks, or made to wear the "drunkard's cloak." This involved the victim being forced to wear a barrel with holes cut out for their arms, legs and head and made to wander around the village or town.

STEALING

Anything worth more than 5 pence was likely to incur the death penalty. Alternatively, the offending hand was chopped off, or the ears and nose . No allowance was made for age, and children as young as 11, such as Alice Glaston (April 13, 1546), were hanged for theft.

Branded for life

In order to keep track of criminal history, Tudors came up with a clever — and very painful — system: branding. Every criminal was marked with a red-hot iron on the hand or wrist. The iron was in the shape of a letter, and each letter represented a certain type of crime. For instance, "M" was for manslaughter and "T" stood for thief.

Though if you had a bit of cash, there was a get-out clause: if you could afford to pay 13 pence (roughly the price of a pair of new shoes), the branding iron would NOT be heated before being pressed on your skin. Which improved the criminal record immensely...

At court, the Justice of Peace decided whether a defendant was guilty and how they were to be punished. And yes, they did look a bit like a wedding cake.

Posh penalty

The most popular punishment in Tudor times was undoubtedly death. Offenders were either burned at the stake, hanged, drawn and quartered, suspended in chains until dead and rotted, or executed.

Most commonly, criminals faced hanging. For the law-breaking nobility, being hanged was far too common. Instead, they had the privilege of having their heads chopped off. Unfortunately, this didn't always go according to plan...

Botched Beheading

Margaret Pole (May 27, 1541)

There are two versions of how Pole died — both nasty. According to one, she was executed by an inexperienced axman who missed her neck the first time, gashing her shoulder; it apparently took a further 10 blows to finish her off.

The second account tells of how she managed to escape from the block and that she was chopped down by the executioner as she ran away from him.

Mechanical Marvels of the Modern Age

Kind killing

When they were introduced, both the guillotine and the electric chair were praised as civilized methods of execution.

Well, you might expect as we get nearer our own times that crime and punishment became a lot more civilized. Welcome to the late 18th and early 19th centuries, when many wonderful inventions made lives more comfortable. And even deaths. Well, in theory, anyway.

Dr. Guillotin, I presume

The guillotine was a tall wooden frame at the top of which was a weighted blade, held by a rope. The condemned person was secured at the bottom of the frame with their head directly below the blade. The blade was released and with one "whoosh" it severed the head from the body.

In 1789, a revolution swept through France which removed the king and nobles from power. On October 10, 1789, Dr. Joseph-Ignace Guillotin, a French physician and inventor of the guillotine, persuaded the government to adopt his device for beheading as a swift and humane method. The new invention soon caught on, particularly as the revolution became more violent. As many as 16,000–40,000 people were killed in this way.

Trust me, Madame. I am a doctor.

24

The guillotine remained in use in France until 1981, when the death penalty was abolished.

One of Dr. Guillotin's most famous "patients" was the King of France himself, Louis XVI, in 1793. Once the King had been beheaded in a matter of seconds, the youngest of the guards seized his bodiless head and held it aloft to show the bloody trophy to the people.

Early electrocutions

Electricity was a wonderful invention of the nineteenth century. Can you imagine a world without all the electrical appliances we have — TV, the Internet, video games...? We can hear you shudder. It has also been used as a means of executing murderers. It was first used in the United States in 1890 when a convicted murderer, William Kemmler, was strapped into a chair and electrocuted. Unfortunately it took a bit of guesswork as to how many volts would be needed to kill him. Several attempts were required, resulting in an eight-minute ordeal that shocked the spectators.

Le Guillotin

If you'd just like to place your head here, Your Majesty. Please observe the safety precautions, as there is a trip hazard.

Today, only certain states in the United States still use this method of execution. Convicts on death row can choose between it and a lethal injection.

Vengeful Victorians

Impersonating a pensioned retired soldier could get you into a lot of trouble in Victorian times...

The Victorian era lasted from 1837 until 1901. During this time, the population in the UK grew at an astounding rate, and in order to keep control, Victorians introduced strict laws. More than 222 crimes were punishable by death, including going out at night with a blackened face and impersonating a pensioned retired soldier. Even lesser punishments than death were not for the faint-hearted...

Transportation

When Victorian prisons began to overflow, criminals started to be shipped out of the country. Britain had a vast empire at the time, which covered most of the world. These new territories were always in need of men to build roads

Send me a postcard!

CHILD CRIMINALS

Unlike today, children in Victorian times were punished just as harshly as adults for their crimes. Here are some cases of child criminals, all convicted in Newcastle upon Tyne in 1871. How do you think each of them was punished?

Case A

Name: Jane Farrell

Age: 12

Crime: Stealing a pair of boots

Case B

Name: Richard Rimmington

Age: 15

Crime: Stealing a pipe

Case C

Name: Henry Leonard Stephenson

Age: 12

Crime: Housebreaking

Punishments:

1: Fourteen days hard labor.

2: Two months in prison.

3: Ten days hard labor.

Answers on page 30!

Source: Tyne and Wear Museums and Archives

and towns. The favorite destination for convicts was Australia. Between 1787 and 1868, more than 160,000 people were shipped there.

Some of those transported committed crimes we still punish today, such as stealing, but some were distinctly odd and probably not that offensive: stealing roots, trees, or plants, or stealing a shroud from a grave. Basically, Victorians used transportation to get rid of anyone they thought was "undesirable."

Treadmill

The treadmill was a giant cylinder with wooden slats. Using the slats as steps, convicts had to climb the treadmill nonstop. It was basically like an ever-revolving set of stairs. Some of the treadmills could accommodate 40 people at a time. Wooden partitions separated the prisoners so they couldn't waste their breath chatting to one another. If they had any breath left, that is.

School and Punishment

Teacher on trial

In 1922, a schoolboy's father decided to sue a teacher for caning his son. This backfired slightly when the judge ruled the teacher had been right to cane the boy. He then ruled that rather than the teacher, the father and his son deserved to be punished!

You may already think that having to go to school is enough of a punishment. But let us prove you wrong. Historically, schools have had ways of enforcing discipline with some rather interesting penalties...

Vicious Victorian schools

There was no pity shown for Victorian pupils who did not perform well. They were sat in a corner with a large cone–shaped hat on their heads with the letter "D" for "dunce" on it. Some children had heavy logs tied to their backs or were made to kneel on the hard wooden floors for hours on end. And if you'd been really, REALLY naughty, then you would be placed in the punishment basket. This was a wickerwork basket in which the child was placed and then hoisted by ropes and pulleys up to the ceiling. Top of the class. Literally.

The cane

Twentieth-century torture

In the 1900s, the cane became the favorite instrument for punishment. It was made out of birch wood or bamboo. Boys would be beaten on the backside and girls on the hands or the backs of their legs. And what crimes had these terrible children committed? Laziness, not telling the truth, and skipping school. Yes, it's hard to believe that schoolchildren could be so evil. The cane was eventually abolished in the 1960s.

The "tawse" or leather strap was another favorite with the teachers, though unsurprisingly not so popular with the children. The tawse was a broad piece of leather that had its end cut into strips. It was used to whip disobedient pupils' hands, and the thin strips would leave some very sore marks indeed. In the UK, the use of the tawse in state schools was abolished in the 1980s, along with all other forms of corporal punishment.

The only time you might see a tawse today is on display in a museum.

Glossary

Athens: an ancient city in Greece where democracy is believed to have begun. Nowadays, it is the capital of Greece

attorney: a person who represents someone in a court of law

Aztecs: an ancient American Indian civilization that lived in present-day Mexico

banished: sent to live far away from your home

brazier: a stand for holding burning coals

bribe: to persuade someone to do something by giving them gifts or money

cangue: a large wooden board placed around the neck

conquer: to take control of a place by force

crucifixion: nailing or tying a victim to a cross

democracy: giving all citizens a say in how the country should be governed

diplomatic: to be sensitive and considerate

execute: to carry out a death sentence

flay: to remove a person's skin

flog: to punish someone by whipping them

gibbet: a wooden structure for hanging people

guillotine: a machine with a heavy blade, used to behead people

legal code: a written statement of laws

Medieval: of the Middle Ages – roughly 500–1500 CE

nobles: rich people who held power

ordeal: a method that was used in Medieval times to prove one's innocence

sarcastic: using ironic statements

sentence: to announce a punishment

Socrates: a philosopher and teacher in ancient Greece

Sparta: an important city-state in ancient Greece that reached the height of its power in 5th century BCE

swineherd: a person who tends to pigs

tawse: a leather strap used to punish schoolchildren

transportation: sent to the colonies of the British Empire

treadmill: a giant cylinder with wooden slats or steps

Answers (p. 27):

Case A: punishment 3

Case B: punishment 1

Case C: punishment 2

More information

Places to visit

Alcatraz Island National Park, San Francisco, California

Anyone can visit America's most famous island prison, also known as "The Rock." Not used as a prison since 1963, today it's a national park open for tours and it is also a wildlife sanctuary. http://www.nps.gov/alca/index.htm

Crumlin Road Gaol, Belfast, UK

The Crumlin Road Gaol in Northern Ireland opened in 1845 and remained a working prison until 1996. Nowadays it is open to the public for tours. www.crumlinroadgaol.com

Jedburgh Castle and Jail, Jedburgh, UK

This Scottish prison was built in 1823, and is unique in that it looks like a castle. Tour the cells and marvel at the exhibition of 19th century prison-related artifacts. www.museumsgalleriesscotland.org.uk/member/jedburgh-castle-jail-and-museum

London Dungeon, London, UK

Along with similar dungeons in Edinburgh, Blackpool, and York, this is one of the more fun ways of exploring crime and punishment through the ages. www.thedungeons.com/

Websites

http://score.rims.k12.ca.us/score_lessons/colonial_court/html/colonial.html

Learn about early America crime and punishment from this website about colonial Virginia.

www.twmuseums.org.uk

Tyne and Wear archives have a unique collection of mug shots of child criminals, their crimes and their punishments.

Publisher's note to educators and parents: Our editors have carefully reviewed these websites to ensure that they are suitable for students. Many websites change frequently, however, and we cannot guarantee that a site's future contents will continue to meet our high standards of quality and educational value. Be advised that students should be closely supervised whenever they access the Internet.

Books

The Gruesome Truth About... (series) by Jillian Powell, Wayland (2012)

Past in Pictures – Crime and Punishment by Alex Woolf, Wayland (2013)

Index